The Stew Crew

The Stew Crew

Ankye Sunoman

XULON ELITE

Xulon Press Elite
2301 Lucien Way #415
Maitland, FL 32751
407.339.4217
www.xulonpress.com

© 2023 by Ankye Sunoman

All rights reserved solely by the author. The author guarantees all contents are original and do not infringe upon the legal rights of any other person or work. No part of this book may be reproduced in any form without the permission of the author. The views expressed in this book are not necessarily those of the publisher.

Due to the changing nature of the Internet, if there are any web addresses, links, or URLs included in this manuscript, these may have been altered and may no longer be accessible. The views and opinions shared in this book belong solely to the author and do not necessarily reflect those of the publisher. The publisher, therefore, disclaims responsibility for the views or opinions expressed within the work.

Paperback ISBN-13: 978-1-66287-356-0
Ebook ISBN-13: 978-1-66287-357-7

In memory of you, sis! You left me too soon!
Making you proud here on Earth!

Heidi Strobel (1981-2019)

Dedication:

I WOULD FIRST like to dedicate this book to my kids. You are my drive to work so hard toward my dreams. I hope by watching me achieve them, it gives you the courage to always reach for the stars. I love all seven of you very much!

To Martin Young, thank you for loving me and supporting me through this fun adventure of reaching my dreams. Without it, *The Stew Crew* would still just be a dream. I love you!

A special thank you to my friend, Ashley, for the idea of writing a cookbook and incorporating my art into it. That small suggestion turned into a great big idea. Thank you for the push in the right direction. Without you, this book would not be possible!

Last, but not yeast, to my special friend, Connie. All of those puns are turtley all for yew! I know how much you clove them.

Hello! It is so nice to meet you! You may have heard of me. If you haven't that is okay. I love meeting new people! My name is Ankye. What is your name? Oh! Fantastic! That really is a lovely name. I am looking forward to being your friend!

I am the keeper of a very special magical garden, hidden away in a magical forest where gnomes and fairies live. They help me tend the garden where we grow all sorts of vegetables, fruits, and herbs which we use in our many different recipes. We have lots of fun coming up with new recipes that not only taste great, but can feed many!

We use our recipes to spread love around the world. Love is the main ingredient in our recipes. It just makes the food taste so much better if you are cooking food to share with others.

Are you ready to meet The Stew Crew? I know you will grow to love them because they were grown to love you! But before we get started, I just want to go over a few things that will make your cooking experience easier and safer.

If you are new to cooking and under the age of eighteen, please get your parents' permission before cooking. Just in case they need to be there to supervise and help along the way.

The Stew Crew is not responsible for how your soup turns out. You may not have the same results they have. You may live in a different part of the world, like in the mountains or by the ocean, which means your altitude will be different and can affect the outcome. You may be new to cooking, while they have cooked for many years, or your ingredients can vary based on where you live.

All of these soups can be cut in half by using half of the amount of the ingredients the recipes call for. If a recipe calls for ten potatoes, use five. If a recipe calls for twelve cups of vegetable stock, use six, and so on. If there are leftovers, we freeze ours in a freezer-safe Ziploc bag. Be sure to lay it on its side in a baking pan. Once frozen, we can stack them easier for storage. This allows more room in the freezer to stock up for the winter.

You will want to use a soup pot. We use a 16 quart when cooking the full recipe. You can use a smaller one if you only do half the amount.

Last but not least, always wash your hands and your vegetables before you get started cooking.

Well, I have lots of work to get done today! Please have fun cooking these recipes and getting to know The Stew Crew. I know they are excited to meet you! They have eagerly, but patiently waited for this day. Much love and peace on this glorious day!

Love,

Table of Recipes

"Mama Mia" Meatball Soup 1

"Everything, but the Kitchen Sink" Stew 5

"Fly the Coop" Chicken-N-Noodles 9

"Philly Me Up" Steak Soup 13

Broccoli and Cauliflower "Show Me the Cheddar" Soup 17

"Appeeling" Potato Soup 21

"Rootin'-Tootin'" Chili 25

"Mama Mia" Meatball Recipe 29

"Easy Peasy" Egg Noodles 31

"Mama Mia" Meatball Soup

Cooked by: Chef Cali

Hiya! I have been waiting for this day for what seems like ages. I am so excited to get to show you how to make my "Mama Mia" Meatball Soup. My soup has a few more steps, but it is just as easy to make as the recipes from the rest of The Stew Crew. You may be wondering about The Stew Crew and just who we are. Well, let me give you a quick rundown before we get started making our delicious soup.

The Stew Crew started many years ago. We were grown in a very secret magical garden called Ankye's garden where fairies and gnomes tended to us as we grew. One day, a fairy used her magic wand and made some of the vegetables come to life! These vegetables became known as The Stew Crew, and it was our job to help Ankye come up with recipes filled with love that would help spread love throughout the world from the inside out.

There are seven of us that are in charge of the soup recipes: Broclynn, Tommy, Olivia, Que, Mash, Carl, and I. We share the recipes that have been handed down to us from our ancestors and we also like to create new soups to share with the world, spreading love one recipe at a time! The seven of us decided to call ourselves The Stew Crew.

That is how we came to be. Ankye tells a much better version of it, but that is for another time. We must get on with sharing our soups, so let's get to our kitchens and make sure we have our ingredients ready. Last one there is a rotten egg!

Ingredients:

2 lbs. Meatballs
*Follow meatball recipe on page 29. Store bought or pre-made meatballs work also. If raw, they will need to be cooked first.

1 lb. Bacon
12 Cups Beef Stock
8 Cups Milk
5 Cups Shredded Cheese
½ Stick Butter

4 Garlic Cloves, minced or chopped
4 Cups Diced Potatoes
3 Carrots, chopped
3 Celery Stalks
1 Medium Onion

- **First Step: Wash them veggies**

It is always important to wash your vegetables before putting them in your recipes. Give them a good scrubbing and rinse them off, then pat them dry.

- **Second Step: Making the Meatballs vs. Pre-Cooked Meatballs**

If you are on a time crunch, it is okay to use pre-cooked or pre-made meatballs. You can even make the meatballs beforehand and freeze them until you are ready to use them in this recipe. If you are going to make them by hand, turn your oven on to 350 degrees so it can pre-heat, then let's head on over to page 28. Follow the directions and then we will meet back here when you are done for the third step.

- **Third Step: Chop and boil the vegetables**

Wow, you are fast! Now that you have your meatballs cooking or ready and set to the side until later, we are going to get the vegetables ready for the soup pot.

First, peel the carrots and chop them up.

Next, you can peel the potatoes or leave the skin on them, the choice is yours. Chop them up and put them with the carrots.

Next, chop up the celery and the onion and add them to the carrots and potatoes. You can mince the garlic or chop it up at this time, but set it to the side to add it to the soup later.

Now get a pot of water and boil the veggies (**go to the fourth step while the veggies are cooking**). When the potatoes are soft, drain and set to the side.

- **Fourth Step: It's bacon time!**

Now is a great time to cook up the bacon! First, if you are still cooking those meatballs, check on them and set them to the side if they are done. If your meatballs are already ready, don't worry about this step. Fry up the bacon on medium heat in a frying pan. Once the bacon has cooled off, you can chop it up and set it to the side.

- **Fifth Step: Get out that soup pot!**

It is time to put our soup together. Get out your soup pot (a 16 quart is a great size for most soup recipes). Turn your stove on to medium heat and let's start adding those ingredients. Add the milk, the beef stock, the boiled vegetables, the garlic cloves, and a stick of butter. Let it simmer on low heat for about 30 minutes, stirring frequently so the milk does not burn to the bottom or overflow onto the stove.

- **Sixth Step: Adding the meat and cheese**

Let's add the cheese and stir it in until melted fully. Then add the bacon and the meatballs and let the soup simmer on low heat for about an hour. Stirring every 5 to 10 minutes to make sure nothing is burning to the bottom.

That's a wrap! You may add salt and pepper or garlic seasoning to the soup for more flavor if needed.

Remember to share your soup with someone you love. I am sharing mine with my niece and nephew. They are great and I love being their aunt! They love my recipes and they have even helped me invent a few new ones. Kids sure are creative when it comes to trying and doing new things.

Well, I hope you had a fun time cooking with me! I sure enjoyed cooking with you! Until next time, always remember that nothing is impastable.

Love,

Cali

"Everything, but the Kitchen Sink" Stew

Cooked by: Chef Que

Hello! My name is Chef Que and I am so happy to be showing you how to make my Everything, but the Kitchen Sink Stew. I love to cook; it has been my passion since I was growing on a vine in Ankye's garden. I have been making this soup for many years, but I still like to change it up and try different things. Sometimes I like to replace the potatoes in the stew with sweet potatoes, or maybe you want to try both regular and sweet potatoes in it! That is what is great about this soup, you can play around and experiment and make it your own soup! That is what cooking is all about! Experimenting with different flavors. Try changing the black beans to kidney beans or garbanzo beans! If you don't eat meat, you can leave the meat out of it and use vegetable stock instead. This soup is also great with chicken or ground turkey! The possibilities are endless!

Okie dokie, if you have all of your ingredients out and ready, let us get to the kitchen and I will show you how to make this very simple yummy stew.

Ingredients:

These are the ingredients we will be using today in our stew, unless you need to substitute or change it up. Just use the same amount if you make any changes. For example, if you change the potatoes to sweet potatoes, still use four sweet potatoes.

4 Potatoes (peeled and diced, or if you prefer the skin on, leave the skin on and just dice them up)

4 Carrots, peeled and chopped

4 Celery Stalks, chopped

1 Medium Purple Onion, diced

1 Can Diced Tomatoes (or) **1 ½ Cups** Fresh Diced Tomatoes

2 Cans Corn (or) **3 Cups** Frozen or Fresh Corn

2 Cans Peas (or) **3 Cups** Frozen or Fresh Peas

2 Cans Green Beans (or) **3 Cups** Frozen or Fresh Green Beans

2 Cans Black Beans (or) Garbanzo or Kidney beans

12 Cups Beef Broth or Vegetable Broth (use Chicken Broth if you are using Ground Chicken or Turkey)

½ Stick Butter

2 Cups Spaghetti Sauce

2 lbs. Ground Beef or Ground Turkey or Chicken (or) no meat if vegetarian (**I like to add 4 diced sweet potatoes to the stew for the vegetarian option**)

4 Garlic Cloves, minced (i**f you do not have a garlic mincer, you can simply chop up the fresh garlic**)

1 Tbsp. of each:
- Onion Powder
- Garlic Powder
- Salt & Pepper

Now that we have gone through the ingredients, let me stop and talk to you about the salt and peppering of this stew. You can add salt and pepper to your liking, but make sure not to over salt or over pepper the stew! Just add it in small pinches until you are satisfied with the taste! Or leave it out all together and let those enjoying the stew add what they want to their bowl of stew. You can always add more, but you cannot take it away once too much has been added. All right, let us put the stew together.

- **First Step: Preparing our vegetables**

Remember to always wash your vegetables first. Peel your carrots. Then chop up the onion, garlic, carrots, and celery. Peel (or don't peel) and chop up the potatoes. Turn the stove on medium heat and get out your soup pot (I like to use a 16 quart soup pot). Add the ½ stick of butter to the soup pot and all of the vegetables you just prepared. Let simmer on the stove, stirring occasionally until the onions are soft and a little golden brown around the edges.

- **Second Step: Adding our vegetables to the soup pot**

Next, get out your can opener and open all of the cans of vegetables listed in the ingredients. If you are using frozen or fresh vegetables, just wash and add them. Pour them all into a colander and rinse them off with warm water, then put them in the soup pot.

- **Third Step: Adding the final ingredients**

Now you are going to add the uncooked ground beef, beef stock, and 2 cups of spaghetti sauce to the soup pot. Stir the ground beef into the soup until it is all crumbled up and mixed in well. If you do not eat meat, then add your vegetable stock here and I recommend replacing the ground beef with diced up sweet potatoes instead. If you do this, then peel and chop up 4 sweet potatoes and add them to the soup pot.

- **Fourth Step: It's seasoning time!**

We are going to add the seasonings on this step. Add the onion powder and garlic powder, add your 2 to 3 pinches of salt and pepper, and stir the seasonings into the soup very well. Make sure you turn your stove to a lower heat to slowly simmer the stew.

Okay! So, most of us chefs like to taste their soup after they put in the seasonings; however, we have to be patient. We will not get to taste this soup until it has been slowly cooking for an hour and a half and the ground beef, turkey, or chicken is cooked thoroughly. To those of you who are not using meat, you can taste test the broth at this time and add more seasoning if you feel it needs a little more. Remember to only add a pinch at a time so as not to over season the stew.

- **Fifth Step: Simmering and stirring the stew**

Continue cooking it on low heat for 1 ½ hours. Stir every 10 to 15 minutes. Make sure you scrape the bottom of the pot and mix it around well, so it cooks evenly and does not burn on the bottom of the soup pot.

- **Sixth Step: Taste testing time!**

Now you can taste test the soup. Blow on it first so you don't burn your tongue! Add more seasoning if you feel it is needed. I usually need to add a little more garlic powder and salt to mine, so I do it a pinch at a time until I am satisfied with the flavor. If you are satisfied with the flavor, serve up your soup and be sure to share your soup with someone you love!

I will be sharing mine with my very special friend who I am going to ask to marry me tonight! I sure hope Penny says yes! I have loved her from my head to-ma-toes since we were no bigger than a grasshopper on a vine in Ankye's garden.

I have really enjoyed making my stew with you today! I hope you have, as well! Please have fun with it and change it up to make it your own stew! Experiment with flavors! Until next time, stew unto others as you would have them stew unto you!

Love,

Que

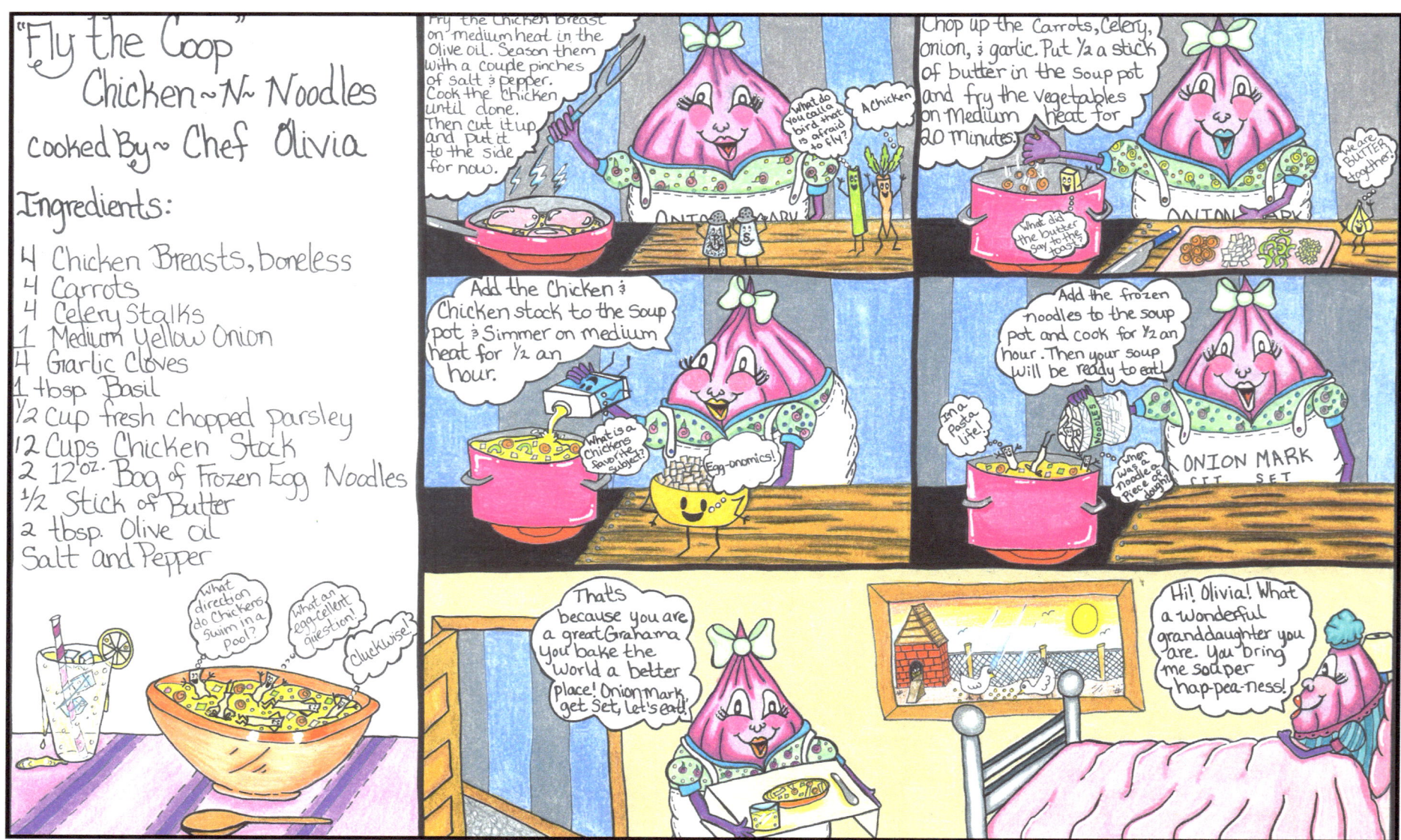

"Fly the Coop" Chicken-N-Noodles

Cooked by: Chef Olivia

Hey, y'all! I am so happy to meet you! I just love soup cook-offs! I love sharing my special soup with everyone I can! My grandma taught me how to cook this soup when I was growing in Ankye's garden! It is where I met Chef Tommy, who y'all will meet later on! He was growing above me on a vine and we have been best friends ever since!

Well, that is probably enough chit chat. I could talk all day about the good ole days in Ankye's garden. Do y'all have your ingredients laid out and ready to go? Let's go down the list and double check to make sure it is all ready! I will meet you in the kitchen!

Ingredients:

4 Chicken Breasts, boneless and skinless
4 Carrots, peeled and chopped
4 Celery Stocks, chopped
1 Medium Yellow Onion, chopped
4 Garlic Cloves, minced or chopped
4 Tbsp. Basil
½ Cup Fresh Parsley, chopped
12 Cups Chicken Stock
2 Bags (12 oz.) Egg Noodles (or you can make your own egg noodles. A bonus noodle recipe is added in the book on page 31)
½ Stick Butter
2 Tbsp. Olive Oil
Salt and Pepper, for taste

- **First Step: Frying up the chicken**

Get a frying pan and turn the stove on to the medium heat setting. Add your olive oil to the pan and let it heat up for about 2 minutes. Wash your chicken breasts off in cold water and pat dry with paper towels (**Please make sure they are dry before adding them to the oil. Hot oil and water will make a popping reaction and can be dangerous if the oil is too hot**).

Put your chicken breasts into the pan and cook them until fully cooked. Flip them every 5 minutes to prevent them from burning (**While the chicken is cooking, jump to the second step, but remember to stop every 5 mins and flip the chicken**). The juices will run clear and when they are cut open there will be no pink in them. Or for those who have a meat thermometer, the chicken should be cooked to 165 degrees. Once cooled off, shred or chop up the chicken and set to the side.

Now there is another way to cook your chicken, y'all, if you do not want to fry them in olive oil. You can add your chicken and chicken broth together in a pot and boil the chicken until it is 165 degrees. Then you just take the chicken out, shred or chop it up, then put the chicken back in the broth. When you're done with the second step, you can go to the third step and add your chicken and chicken broth to the soup pot with the vegetables.

- **Second Step: While the First Step is cooking, let's prepare the vegetables**

Wash your vegetables very well. Peel the carrots and chop or shred them, whichever you prefer to do. Chop up the celery, onion, and garlic. Then get out your soup pot, add half a stick of butter, and add the chopped up vegetables. Fry them until the edges of the onions are lightly brown.

- **Third Step: Adding the chicken ingredients**

Add the chicken and the chicken broth to the soup pot with the vegetables and simmer on low heat for 1 ½ hours, stirring every once in a while to make sure nothing is sticking to the bottom of the pan.

- **Fourth Step: Adding the noodles and herbs**

For this step, we are adding the noodles. If you use the premade noodles, you can add them now. If you are using the homemade noodles from the bonus recipe on page 31, you can make them up while the soup is simmering during that 1 ½ hours. **Take the time to make the homemade noodle recipe. It really makes the soup even more full of love and flavor.** Then add them to the soup pot at this time. Add the basil and chopped parsley, and continue to simmer for 30 minutes to an hour.

- **Fifth Step: Time to serve up our soup**

You can serve it over mashed potatoes, which is my favorite way to eat them. You can also just have it plain or with crackers on top! Make sure to share it with someone you love!

Our time together went by so fast! I cannot believe it has come to an end already! I am sharing my soup with my Grandma Vedalia! I really enjoy listening to her stories. She is so full of wisdom and I have lots to learn from her!

I hope to see you all again real soon. Until then, let your love grow onion on for all!

Love,

Olivia

"Philly Me Up" Steak Soup

Cooked by: Chef Tommy

Hello! It is so great to see you today! I am really looking forward to making my soup with you! It has been passed down to me from my Grandfather Tony, who says it has been in the family for many years. Olivia, who has been my friend since I was a little yellow bud on my family's Roma tomato vines that grew abundantly in Ankye's garden over the years, says this is one of her favorite soups that I make! I also make a great tomato soup, but that is a recipe for another time.

All right, let us get this party started! Let's go to the kitchen and get our ingredients ready.

Ingredients:

- **2 lbs.** Carne Asada Steak, chopped up
- **1 lb.** Bacon
- **½ Stick** Butter
- **1 Medium** Onion
- **1** Red Bell Pepper
- **1** Green Bell Pepper
- **1** Yellow Bell Pepper
- **1** Orange Bell Pepper
- **3** Potatoes
- **16 oz.** Cream Cheese
- **12 Cups** Beef Stock
- **8 Cups** Milk
- **6 Cups** Mozzarella Cheese
- **4** Garlic Cloves, minced or chopped
- **1 Tbsp.** Seasoning Salt
- **1 Tbsp.** Pepper
- **1 Tbsp.** Garlic Powder
- **1 Tbsp.** Onion Powder

- **First Step: Preparing the vegetables, chopping the bacon, and adding the seasonings**

Get out your soup pot and set it on the stove, but do not turn the stove on just yet. Chop up your uncooked bacon and set to the side for the second step. Wash your vegetables all nice and clean. Peel and chop up the potatoes into tiny bite-sized pieces. Chop up the onion and all of the colorful bell peppers (be sure to clean the seeds out of the peppers as you chop them up). They can be chopped up into whatever size you prefer your peppers to be. Some like big pieces of peppers. I prefer tinier pieces of peppers in my soup. This is all up to you and what you like. Chop up the garlic or mince it with your mincer. Now you may turn your stove on medium heat. Then add the ½ stick of butter to the soup pot, the seasonings, and the vegetables. Fry them until the onions are soft around the edges.

- **Second Step: Carne asada and bacon time!**

Once the peppers and onions have started to become soft, but not quite brown around the edges, add the bacon and cook for about 10 minutes, then add the carne asada to the pan and stir frequently (every 5 minutes, at least) until it is no longer pink.

- **Third Step: Draining the grease**

*Use caution! Very hot! Have assistance with this step if it is needed, please!**

Put a piece of tinfoil in a bowl, put your colander in the bowl, and drain the grease. **Do not rinse it or you will lose all that flavor!** Let the grease cool before pulling out the tinfoil and throw it in the trash.

- **Fourth Step: Beef stock time**

In this step you can add the beef broth to the soup pot and let the potatoes cook. Stir every 10 minutes or so until they are soft (you should be able to put a fork through them and they slide right off). This should take about 30 minutes.

- **Fifth Step: Show us the dairy!**

Add the milk, the cream cheese, and the mozzarella cheese. Stir it in until it is all melted and the soup is all mixed up and creamy! This should take about 15 minutes. You can simmer on low heat for another 15 minutes or 30 minutes if you like to make sure all of the flavors have cooked together, just as long as you stir it. Make sure to scrape the bottom of the pot so nothing sticks and burns to it.

- **Sixth Step: To bread bowl or not to bread bowl? That is the question!**

Get your bread bowls ready! You don't have to use bread bowls, regular bowls work also. You can sprinkle croutons on top with a little extra cheese and a dollop of sour cream and it is still fabulous! I went to my local baker's this time and picked up some pre-made bread bowls. You can also make them homemade if you know how!

Well, you all, I have had a great time! Remember to share your soup with someone you love, it just makes it taste better. I am sharing mine with my twin sister Toma by the river today! She is a food critic and always so honest about how it tastes, sometimes too honest! I am hoping she will approve and it will win the soup cook-off this weekend! I am glad Cali and Broclynn came up with this idea! Fun times with some great friends!

Until next time, I beleaf in you because you are one in a melon!

Love,

Tommy

Broccoli and Cauliflower "Show Me the Cheddar" Soup

Cooked by: Chef Broclynn

Hey, you terrific, wonderful beings! I am so happy to get to spend some time with you and show you my very special soup today! I have been cooking this soup for a really long time. I cooked it for my kids and now I cook it for my grandkids! They get so excited when they know Grandma is in the kitchen cooking her famous soup! I have been dying to share it with others, which is why I had the soup cook-off idea! I am glad that Cali was so quick to agree with it! Ankye picked us on the same day and we instantly hit it off on our way to Ankye's kitchen; we have been the best of friends ever since!

Well, you fantastic peeps! We should get on with it! Follow me to the kitchen and we will get our work area ready to go and double check all of the ingredients.

Ingredients:

- **1 Bag (32 oz.)** Frozen Broccoli (or) **2 lbs.** Fresh Broccoli
- **1 Bag (32 oz.)** Frozen Cauliflower (or) **2 lbs.** Fresh Cauliflower
- **3** Carrots
- **3** Celery Stalks
- **1 Medium** Yellow Onion
- **1 lb.** Bacon
- **3 Cups** Diced Ham
- **12 Cups** Vegetable Stock
- **8 Cups** Milk
- **6 Cups** Shredded Sharp Cheddar Cheese
- **4** Garlic Cloves, minced or chopped
- **1 Container (16 oz.)** Sour Cream

- **First Step: Prepping our vegetables**

Always make sure you wash your vegetables and rinse them very well. Chop up the onion, peel and chop up the carrots, and chop up your celery. Next you will mince your garlic. If you do not have a mincer, that is quite all right, you can simply chop up your fresh garlic.

Get out a pan and turn your stove on to medium heat and add the chopped up vegetables. We are going to fry them until the onions have a light golden brown around the edges.

- **Second Step: Get out the soup pot**

Add the vegetable stock to the soup pot. Then add the veggies that have been frying and add them to the soup pot. Next add the frozen or fresh broccoli to the pot. Cook on medium heat and cook until the broccoli and cauliflower are tender, about 45 minutes to an hour. **While the veggies get tender, go on to the third step, please!**

- **Third Step: It is bacon time!**

***If you do not eat meat, you can skip this step! You do not have to add meat to make this soup great! It is great without it!**

Get out a frying pan and turn the stove on to medium heat. Cook up the bacon, then let it cool. While the bacon is cooling, cook up the chopped up ham for about 10 minutes in the bacon grease. Put on a paper towel when done to soak up extra grease, then pat dry. Once the bacon has cooled off, you can chop it up, as well, then add it to the soup pot.

- **Fourth Step: Dairy say the next step?!**

Time to add the milk and the sour cream to the soup pot. Mix well until the sour cream is fully mixed in.

- **Fifth Step: Let's make it cheesy!**

For the final step, show me the cheddar! Mix in the shredded cheddar cheese until it is all melted into the soup!

- **Sixth Step: Sharing is caring!**

Find someone to share this delicious soup with! It makes it so much cheddar! I am sharing it with my grandsons, Steven and Samuel. They should be over any minute!

Thank you so much for sharing part of your day with me! I had so much fun making my soup with you! I sure hope you had a good time and enjoyed this soup! We will see you at the soup cook-off, where it is not just about winning for me, it is about sharing my love through a good bowl of soup!

Until next time, remember there is nothing cheddar than sharing!

Love,

Broclynn

"Appeeling" Potato Soup

Cooked by: Chef Mash

Hello! It is nice to meet you! I am looking forward to showing you how to make my soup! It is quite ap-peeling I hear! Ankye showed me how to cook. She took me under her wing and taught me everything I know. She really is a wonderful being and if you are ever so lucky to get to meet her one day, you will see exactly what I mean. Everything Ankye does, she does with love. Love just makes everything more special! Now I get to take you under my wing and teach you!

I could rattle all day about Ankye and all she is and does, but then we would never get to make this award-winning soup for the cook-off, so let us get to it! Onward to the kitchen, my students!

Ingredients:

10 **Medium** Red Potatoes
3 **Cups** Cubed Ham
1 **lb.** Thick-Cut Bacon
4 Celery Stalks
4 Carrots
1 **Medium** Yellow Onion
12 **Cups** Vegetable Stock
8 **Cups** Milk
6 **Cups** Shredded Cheese
½ **Cup** Fresh Parsley, chopped
5 Garlic Cloves, minced
½ Stick Butter
Salt and Pepper

- **First Step: Prep those veggies!**

Always wash your vegetables before getting started. Pat them dry before chopping them up. Chop up the potatoes, celery, carrots, onion, and parsley, then mince the garlic. Put the onion, garlic, and parsley to the side for now. Put a pot of water on the stove, throw a pinch or two of salt in the pot and turn the stove on medium heat. Boil the potatoes, celery, and carrots. While you are waiting for them to soften, let's go to the second step.

- **Second Step: You bacon me happy!**

Get out a second frying pan and set your stove to medium low and fry up the bacon. Let it cool off, then chop it up. While the bacon is cooling off, you can fry the onions and the garlic in the bacon grease. When the onions are golden brown, lay them on a paper towel to soak up the extra grease.

- **Third Step: Let's ham it up!**

Time for the ham to shine! You can buy pre-cubed ham or you can buy a ham and cut it into cubes yourself. You can also use leftover ham maybe from a Sunday dinner or holiday dinner that you have saved in your freezer for a day like today! Just thaw it out the day before you use it in your refrigerator!

*If you do not eat meat, you can leave out all the meat and just add 3 to 4 extra potatoes.

- **Fourth Step: Everything, but the cheese**

Get your soup pot out and turn your stove to medium heat. Add the milk, the vegetable stock, the ham, the vegetables, and the bacon. Add the parsley at this time and a couple pinches (**I usually use 5 pinches**) of salt and pepper. Simmer to a low boil, stirring frequently so the milk does not burn to the bottom of the pot or boil over the top sides.

- **Fifth Step: Say cheese!**

Add the cheese to the soup and stir it until it is all melted into the soup. If you want to add extra cheese, you may! I like to say, **"You can never be too cheesy."**

Hot dog! It is time! This next step is the most important and is my favorite part of the soup. Eating it with someone you love! I am sharing my soup with my one and only favorite tater on this planet: Mary! Mary has been by my side since we were little eyes being planted in the ground by the one and only Ankye herself. Mary and I loved listening to Ankye sing and tell us stories as we grew in her garden.

I had so much fun showing you how to make my soup. I hope you enjoyed it, as well! Enjoy the soup you have made with love! Enjoy the time with the person or people you share it with! Soup is so much better enjoyed with friends and family! I will see you at the soup cook-off! May the best soup win!

Until then, always remember, "Spread hap-pea-ness everywhere you go!"

Love,

Mash

"Rootin'-Tootin'" Chili

Cooked by: Chef Carl

Howdy, y'all! I am speechless! I cannot believe you are standing here in front of me! I have been waiting on this day for what seems like ages. Ankye told me this day would come and I didn't believe it, but I'll be corn chowder! Here you are, just like she said you would be! We are going to have a "rootin'-tootin'" good time making my soup! I learned to make this soup when I was knee-high to one of those grass hopping bugs. Let's get to the kitchen and get this souper night started by washing our hands!

Ingredients:

- **2 lbs.** Ground Beef
- **2 Cans** Diced Tomatoes
- **4 Cans** Chili Beans
- **2 Cans** Black Beans
- **1 Can** Corn
- **1 Can** Tomato Paste
- **1** Green Bell Pepper
- **1 Medium** Onion
- **4** Garlic Cloves
- **8 Cups** Beef Broth
- **½ Stick** Butter
- **2 Tbsp.** Chili Powder
- **2 Tbsp.** Cumin
- **2 Tbsp.** Onion Powder
- **1 Tbsp.** Salt
- **1 Tbsp.** Pepper

- **First Step: The veggies!**

Chop up your onion, green pepper, and your garlic cloves.

- **Second Step: Let's heat things up!**

Get out your soup pot.

Now, I use my 16 quart soup pot when I make my rootin'-tootin' chili. I like to make as much as possible so I have plenty to share with the ones I love! Heck, I just love everyone! If I had one wish, it would be to share my soup with everyone in the world, so they know how much I love them, even though we have never met! Anyways, I am rambling. Let's get back to the soup pot!

Turn the stove on medium heat, put the half stick of butter into the pot. Add the chopped up green peppers, onions, and garlic cloves into the pot. Fry them up until they are tender and the onions are slightly golden.

- **Third Step: To add or not to add the meat?**

    *If you do not eat meat, you can substitute the meat with sweet potatoes. Just dice up four sweet potatoes and add them at this time.

    If you use the 2 pounds of ground beef, then add it to the soup pot at this time. Continue stirring it so it does not burn on the bottom of the pan until the meat is fully cooked (this means there is no more pink in the meat).

- **Fourth Step: You can do this!**

    Add the beef broth (**or vegetable broth if you do not eat meat**), beans, corn, tomatoes, and tomato paste to the soup pot. Stir it all together!

- **Fifth Step: Spice it up!**

    Add the chili powder, cumin, onion powder, salt, and pepper. You can taste it at this time, but be careful because it may be hot.

    If you need to add more seasoning, then you can at this time, but only a pinch at a time, you hear? If you add too much, you can't take it back! I have made that mistake a time or two. You just keep doing it until you get it right! It took me a year to master my famous rootin'-tootin' chili, but I never gave up. Now, here we are today, I am teaching you how to make it!

    Let simmer for an hour on low heat. Stir frequently and make sure you are scraping the bottom of the pot so none of it burns to the bottom. **Let's go set that table and so we can sit down and talk about our dreams, inspirations, and how well you did making your chili!**

    My friend Al Mond is coming over today to sit and eat with me! I grew up next to him in Ankye's garden. The tree he grew from often shaded me from the harsh sun and extra windy days! We spent our days growing up talking about our dreams and how we would change the world one day! He went on to make pies filled with love, sharing them all over the world. Now, I am finally getting my dream by sharing my recipe with you! What a grand moment!

Thank you so much for sharing this moment with me today! I will see you at the soup cook-off! Until then, always remember, "Team work, makes the bean work" and "Spread that love like butter on toast!"

Love,

Carl

"Mama Mia" Meatball Recipe

Ingredients:

1 **lb.** Ground Beef
1 **lb.** Ground Italian Sausage
1 **Cup** Italian Bread Crumbs
2 Eggs
¼ **Cup** Milk
1 **Tbsp.** Onion Powder
1 **Tbsp.** Garlic Powder
2 **tsp.** Salt and Pepper

- **First Step: Turn up the heat.**

Turn your oven on to 350 degrees. Anytime you are baking or using your oven, it is good to pre-heat it first as it will cut down your cooking time. Pre-heating means letting the inside of the oven get to the temperature the oven is set to, in this case 350 degrees.

- **Second Step: Let's mix things up**

Add all of the ingredients into a mixing bowl and mix together very well.

- **Third Step: Get the scoop**

You can wear gloves for this part if you would like. Scoop 2 tablespoons of the meatball mixture, roll into a ball, and put into a baking pan.

- **Fourth Step: Let's bake!**

Put the meatballs in the oven for 45 minutes to an hour. While waiting for them to cook, let's get back over to the third step of my "Mama Mia" Meatball Recipe (on page ___). I will race you back on the count of 3.

1….2….3! **Last one there is a rotten egg!**

"Easy Peasy" Egg Noodles

Ingredients:

4 Large Eggs

1 ½ tsp. Salt

4 Tbsp. Milk

3-4 Cups All-Purpose Flour

- **First Step: Let's get crackin'**

Mix the eggs and milk into a bowl until it is well mixed. Then mix in the salt and gradually mix in the 3 cups of flour. Add the last cup of flour slowly as needed until the dough is not sticky.

- **Second Step: We all need a rest sometimes**

Let the dough sit in the bowl with saran wrap covering it for 20 minutes to let it rest.

- **Third Step: Making the noodles**

Sprinkle some flour on the countertop you have prepared by cleaning off and sanitizing before starting this step. Roll the dough out onto the floured countertop until it is ¼ inch thick, then cut it into strips. You can cut it into whatever size noodle you would like it to be. I like my noodles to be about half an inch in width and 2 inches in length because I like having lots of noodles in my soup.

- **Fourth Step: Let's add them to the soup**

Now you can add your homemade noodles to the soup when you are ready for that step in Olivia's "Fly the Coop" Chicken-N-Noodles (on page 9).

CPSIA information can be obtained
at www.ICGtesting.com
Printed in the USA
LVHW072107050423
743580LV00002B/4